The Post-Rapture Diner

Also by Dorothy Barresi

All of the Above, 1991

Chapbook

The Judas Clock, 1986

The Post-Rapture Diner

Dorothy Barresi

University of Pittsburgh Press

The publication of this book is supported by grants from the National Endowment for the Arts in Washington, D.C., a Federal agency, and the Pennsylvania Council on the Arts.

Published by the University of Pittsburgh Press, Pittsburgh, Pa. 15261

Manufactured in the United States of America
Printed on acid-free paper
10 9 8 7 6 5 4 3 2

Library of Congress Cataloging-in-Publication Data and acknowledgments of permissions will be found at the end of this book.

A CIP catalogue record for this book is available from the British Library.

Eurospan, London

Book design: Frank Lehner

for Phil, true heart,
and in memory of my mother

Blown hair is sweet, brown hair over the mouth blown,
Lilac and brown hair;
Distraction, music of the flute, stops and steps of the mind
over the third stair

—T. S. ELIOT, "Ash Wednesday"

I'm just dumb enough not to want to be Tarzan all my life.

—JOHNNY WEISMULLER, 1934

And he took the blind man by the hand, and led him out of the town; and when he had spit on his eyes, and put his hands upon him, he asked him if he saw anything.

And he looked up, and said, 'I see men as trees, walking.'

—MARK 8:23, 24

Contents

The Post-Rapture Diner

Some Questions We Might Ask

1

This morning after the earthquake
I lay in bed listening.
First light, and the studs in the walls
and the crossbeams settled down again,
the water pipes and heating ducts,
carpet nails, each
low thing groaning.
                    Cubes began dropping
one by one from the automatic
ice cube maker down the hall.
The electricity in my alarm clock hiccuped off, then on.

2

At what age are we no longer considered
too young to die?
I thought about my sister Ellen.
At thirteen and twelve and fifteen,
she beat me with a fuzzy bedroom slipper,
her eyes gone to bored, peevish discs.
I can't always call it abuse. The lack of love

she had for me had reasons, and those,
reasons of their own.
Still, in low moments, cast down,
I can hate myself without trying, and my decent,
mute, and muddled parents
for the failures she found in me.

      But it wasn't a clear case of anything.
Not like the story of my friend's youngest sister, who,
without language or recourse,

amidst bears and wicker and ruffles, curled
into a brine shrimp—tiny
pink nothing—
each time her father slipped soundlessly from her room.
Years like that.
Then, when words came, years more,
and not one change
or day in the crazy world to tell.

3

Listen. Here is a fact about personal safety
I like to keep in mind.
If a leash or silk tether tied us,
                                        like a sine wave snapped
back from the invisible future,
to everyone who held
our safety in hand: every teacher and lawyer, parent,
crossing guard and fast
food cook, every pharmacist, spot welder, pilot and so on,

we couldn't walk down the street without tripping
and falling on our faces.
After the earthquake this morning
the glass in the windows flexed
subtly, intermittently—
a faint murmur of steel in the day
urging us onward,
and our reluctances,
which is said to be one of the seven
easiest words in the English language to say: *murmur*.

4

I took a drink of water.
Later, doing dishes left from the night before,
I imagined the suds pearlescent
DNA molecules
mounting each other for the steady air.
It occurred to me then: idiot!
I should have crawled under something heavy, my writing desk,
or braced myself upstairs
in the upstanding, rectilinear
safety of a doorway.

5

I'd been surviving by accident all day.
Like this one last theory
buzzing my brain,
that cats and dogs leave home for the scrub

and creosote hills above Sunland and Thousand Oaks
a few days before a temblor hits.
Later, picked up
in record numbers by the county, they're counted,
and after a decent interval,
claimed or gassed;

and the coyotes, too, have their feast.
To know something's coming, anything, sub rosa
in the meat and tender
architecture of our paws!
Of course we have no such wild sense,

but what if we did?
Leave or howl, diminish—on all fours at the concrete river—
where would we go next?
How far away from home is safe?
Face on the river,
who will tell us to stop when we finally arrive?

Mother Hunger and Her Seatbelt

Things are more like they are now than they ever were before.
—Dwight D. Eisenhower

"When my first husband left me
I thought about forgiveness in ways
I hadn't before: I wanted to annihilate the bastard!

Pontiacs reminded me of him.
So did Robert Hass's poems, though not the one
about the gazelle watching his own entrails
being eaten pink by a jackal;
that one was safe.

I owned that poem for a while. And like drink
or pure selfishness,
it got me past those first, virtuoso weeks
of living my life in a provisional way,
not eating a full meal ever, or sleeping past noon

then getting up at 3 A.M. to watch *Amazing Discoveries*
on channel 13.
The one about knives. The one
about hair loss and yellow teeth turning whiter
under the pressure of oxygen.
And I was breathing, too,

coming up for air now and then.
Finally, when I spoke to Father Bentner about
this inability to find—in the face of the only
real injury I'd known not counting
childhood name-calling or petty

family squabbles—Jesus,
he stubbed out his Parliament in a teacup,
rubbed his raw

canonical jawbone, then spoke quietly—no, he intoned—
about the peace that passeth understanding,
Galatians and 'long suffering,'

as though a woman were nothing but a cold fish
and a bit of sourdough
about to undergo the long, late division
feeding multitudes. As though
I were dead already.
Then he asked for a hug and good-bye, grab the surplice,

time to lead a rosary for Saint Lucy's Club.
A hug! Horny old fool.
That afternoon the sun fell
in slices through the trees, red birthday cake, and I
was famous with anger. Shaking.
The trees weren't the usual, Dutch-diseased elms

I'd grown up with,
but pestles grinding down some enormous
aspirin into the earth I couldn't take
for the headache starting
behind by eyebrows.
My Forgiveness Migraine, I call it now.

But back then, what did I know?
Indomitable self-love, city of scorn—any truth
is true enough in a pinch.
So when I saw *it*
flopping in the gutter by my car,
I got the message right away: curbside salvation

like a knock between the shoulder blades. Voilà!
A bluegill, I swear,

lost by an errant sea gull drunk on berries, or simply
blown off course
from Turkeyfoot Lake. Not a keeper, mind you.
Not enough to feed a family of one,

but a dirty four-inch fry the color of Mexican opal
dimming out on dry land.
A fluke, and a token of natural selection which says
the one who flies highest
without proper equipment
gets dropped, dropped, dropped. Just like that

I saw that I, too,
was one of God's poor dumb creatures
trying to make a go of it in the real world,
and death and suffering a factor
in making me feel better about living.
Someone else's death and suffering, that is.

At least that's what I thought then.
Call it my early conclusion.
Now I wonder with the rest, does innocence exist?
Is nature all fucked up?
Uncorrupted, we're worse than metaphysical;
we haven't got a clue. But that afternoon

I went away feeling
a whole lot meaner and better in this world.
Not special, mind you. Not asking
whyme, whyme,
because that's silly. I wasn't a me just then. I was.
Like a baby tooth left dangling from a doorknob,
or a half-sick tree,

or my seatbelt cutting bandolier-style across my chest
to keep me from sinking
into the wide, hot upholstery without recourse,
because *X* really does
mark the spot.

Then for five minutes, maybe ten,
I tuned in the heavy metal stations and drove
and knew where I was going.

Home to eat my young.
Home, where the heart hunkers down into the mud
with the rest of the bottom feeders, then all day,
baleful and sulky,
for what feels like an entire lifetime—guaranteed—
our blood gills work and blaze

and we never need sharpening,
though *blaze, blaze,* we wait also in a darkness
deeper down, like this entreaty
for the obvious miracle to come."

Poem

The enormous courage of the ice cream man
Who has a handcart, bells, no reticence, two soccer games, six

birthday parties, rancheras blaring
from many shouldered estereos,

Who has a park transfused by pink arterial balloons and piñatas
in the shapes of dogs, donkeys, vampires, Bart Simpson, Bart Simpson,

Who has a fixed stare
and both his testicles, PraiseMaryKockWood,

Who has citron and mango and horchata
but no grape today,

no Ninja Turtle popsicles either, dream pop, cream pop,
Who has eaten the radish of happiness

but not the chicken liver of wisdom,
Whose wife loves him,

Pepita, my chubby, my dove, when he comes and who knows, as he does,
that 29th and Main Street meet in hard opposition, wind,

the eucalyptus and palm trees
shake, there are earthquakes, what's real

knocks at the windows but there is nothing more dangerous
than a young man of a certain smiling

sweating disposition with a gun
and no drugs, or some drugs, or it's got

nothing to do with drugs this time but money: some or none.
Who says I have none.

Who says I have none to the occluded front of the young man's face and
the scary movie hard-on gun in the young man's

pocket in his hand—
Give it up old fucker!—the boy's T-shirt reading

"Chaos ain't what it used to be."
Who says to the boy again I have none, nada, zip,

as the vehement tolling of bells at Our Lady of Ectomorphic
Angels on Dust plays on,

Who says no no no until the gun butt and the ravishing
tones in his head make him spin, pants shitted on the way down

so that later when the cops walk away shaking
their pitiful keys to the kingdom, roger and out, they

hold their noses. Who has mixed credit, four grown children, ten
grandchildren, no license for vending, a baseball game, three

late-breaking birthday parties with their grubby dimes
sweat-fisted; Who has sixteen bridesmaids in red satin dresses

and red satin shoes but no photographer—
what the hell?—who say they are hungry, hot, caliente, give us

something for this muy caliente day in which
we have all failed to be killed, PraiseMaryVirginofGuadalupe,

radiant pincushion of Christ.
Who has the Immigration and Naturalization Service.

Who has a thousand borders to cross
not counting Ghetto Boyz, Primera Flats, and the 29th St. Gang

between one curb and the next bump up.
Who has a clean record because there is no record.

Who has a 1973 Dodge Dart Swinger.
Who has a barbecue. Who has two graduations. Who has ninety-three winos

making out shamelessly with the grass.
Who has a handcart, bells, sky, fame, a wife

alternately weeping and sipping from his left nipple
with the tip of her tongue

in their bedroom later, who raises it, the chill,
the chill nipple of the living ice cream man.

My Anger in 1934

The story the body lives in is crazy.
It begins and ends and there is
no end to it but change.

❖

Who was the president in 1934?
Who ran the fastest, held the title?
Who ate radish pudding and green, tinned beef? Who drank
the strong brown god of many beers
behind the canning factory
when their shift was pronounced
dead and dead and over?

Who circled the world in an airplane but lost
his baby to a ladder at the window?

And the rungs of the ladder
that reached so high—you have to believe every one of them
shone with promise and default
like America herself
in 1934. America the beautiful.

I tell you, I have a temper.
It does not mean I have the right to understand it
calmly, or contractually,
as a real estate agent bringing off a deal
for a fixer-upper on a corner lot
with terminal termites—okay—
but what a view!

❖

My father tells a story of 1934.
It is the one I'll tell my shrink

some afternoon when the sun has gone stately
behind the vertical blinds,
and the darkness which ensues is a solid
through a solid,
around a lone *Ficus benjamina,*

and I believe the good doctor has grown fidgety, myself
having bored her to tears . . .

and it goes like this.
Lumped yellow on a bull's-eye plate,
it was the squash he wouldn't eat, no thank you. Or the radio dial

left glowing all night,
until the voice in that disobedient
half-moon named Emerson—how it corresponded
to my father's merciful and true reasons for living
in 1934, with cowboys and pop flies,
the hard out
and Ty Cobb, Ty Cobb,
the long way home though tall grass whistling
Minnie the moocher, she was a lowdown
hootchie-cootcher.

Either way
he would not apologize.
And my grandmother, a thickset Sicilian woman more frightened
of her anger than angry, or perverse,
would not take no for an answer.

It isn't loss I'm writing about for a change.
It isn't charity begins at home.
Just that when a woman takes her oldest son
to the gates of the local orphanage, hefts him up

(he was light as a feather,
a dog's tear),
to carry him the last

gravel-sounding steps toward county doors
(we do not waste in this house!)

and the boy kicking and convulsing out his terror
with no mama, no, no,
it is one of those moments that bestow upon us
something like hindsight:
acid insight.
Then the knowledge of who and what we are
might last generations,
like the contrail of a great ghost fighter plane,
though we do effectively
nothing ever about it.

❖

Don't get me wrong.
History isn't tyranny.
But the bloodline that begins in said parking lot and ends
in Akron, Ohio,
under the winged boot of Goodyear, the Pope,
and the Soap Box Derby,
what can I say about a family like that?
My father twirling Chianti in Depression glass

has a way of telling stories, I tell you,
it would break your heart.
And my sister catches me
across the mouth again
with the back of her hand—shut up, shut up

and listen.
My brother, Tim,
breaks my brother Patrick's collarbone
inadvertently. And Chuck, grown now,
cannot understand why his wife's son loves him.
Not really, he says, *but the thought*
haunts me sometimes. What keeps us
from hurting something small?

History *isn't* tyranny.
In good arms my grandmother lifted my father up,
arms we recognize immediately
from the memory of people punching bread dough down
as though it were their lives.
But that's another story.

In the one I'm telling today, without benefit of shrink,
a boy is twisting, hiccuping,
pleading, as a feather
bluer than midnight
shimmies on the sensible, raging woman's hat:

No mama, *please*.

❖

What then of the progeny in the wings?
The undetonated cherubs, grandchildren and children
waiting to be born
of the blood of the crying boy himself.
What do they have to say
about all this racket?

I'll give you a clue.

Someone count to ten slowly.
Someone twist in the world like an angel/rat
tensing, stomach to the blow.

❖

Somedays, I see my brothers and sister and I
for what we've always aspired to be.
Ordinary wrecked people.
Not pilots lost fifty-odd years over the Atlantic Ocean
only to be found by some fluke of fate
or clearing weather

and deposited
on a runway in real time,

blinking, disavowed,
still wearing our outdated flak jackets
and our enormous, misguided passions.

Never mind.
The sound of an engine turning over
always rescues the hero in America.
Horselaugh, sputter and catch,
the roar that drowns out
all reasonable doubt:

"Hush, I'd never leave you.
Dio mio, hush; you'll wake the dead."

As if that weren't the point.
Then my father is carried exhausted, faint, compliant, sobbing
—barely able to sob—

back to the waiting Nash
to feel the full weight of good in the world,
of which he now is certain.
Unforsakenness!
It is 1934, you see,
the war has not yet begun.
And we are inside the story
this story lives in, waiting to take our lonely turn.

Hush, I'll never leave you.
Hush, a boy is being gently laid
across the backseat's deep green sea of tufted leather.

Called Up: Tinker to Evers to Chance

In three weeks he will be back down talking
drunk in the Econo Lodge
off Sugar Creek Road,

as reported by the *Charlotte Observer:* vowing return.
Not enough heat, pepper, punch & judy.
Occasional hits in the wheelhouse,

but clearly not knocking
the wide moon out of round over Baltimore
or bleary-eyed, noble Detroit.

Luck throws its change-up.
Luck, the old timers say, and who should know better,
with their colons and bum tickers,

their failing vision of which tears are the by-product
in spring when azaleas
and baseball bloom,

luck could throw a lambchop past a wolf.
So it does. It's true. Now
admit it's the very same food chain of love—self-love and self-pity—

we rattle each day
as a weak kind of answer, snarling it
down to the bone with our hungers. We're *still* hungry

for more than words in our mouths. For once,
we want not to be
so replaceable. So the shortstop

is smart in his own dumbfounded way.
He's wearing the gold cross and gold chain
his mother, Lupe, sent last winter

from the Dominican Republic.
He isn't asking any tough questions.
When his name is picked apart

by the P.A.'s rickety static, then boomed
over red clay basepaths
and tobacco barns slotted open

to catch the killer sun,
and Neatsfoot Oil making the gloves glisten and the ball
smack! smack! like ripe, dangerous

fruit in their hands,
he sails his cap high up: the thing wanted—
it was all *worth* wanting. As for what will hurt him

most cruelly in the end, hope
ending or hope beginning
all over again like some cosmic, half-baked

karmic plan for winning
despite the cost,
it's academic, really. It's in the air like sweat, or smoke,

or pine tar pitch,
or that other story we keep feeding ourselves.
The one about the bug being born

into the body of the president, and
later, into a gleaming white twenty-gallon hat.

It's never too early for regret.
Look. Already the crowd is singing "Rocky Top," and swaying
as the great, right boy who's grinning

sneezes once, waves
back to the wartime geezers—adíos!—
then runs down the dugout steps and out of sight.

The Post-Rapture Diner

A thought you cannot call back,
and empty shoes like
exclamation points
on every road from here to Tucson.

Who will knock their boots against the doorjamb now
and enter shyly?
Who will peel the vegetables?
Pie domes cloud over. Old sugar

makes a kind of weather in there—
webbed, waiting.
Tiers of doughnuts go woozy with collapse.

We deed and we will.
We bow to what providence we understand
and cede the rest: our lies and doubts, our human,
almost necessary
limitations. *Probably I should have,*

we whispered more than once, shaking our heads.
Probably. Now what's left of the past
hangs in a walk-in freezer,
fat-shrouded, bluing,

and all we know of the present
is a spatula in a coffee can
on a cold grill, pointing to heaven.

When I Think About America Sometimes (I think of Ralph Kramden)

raising that truncheon of an arm
to shake it, ham-handed and heavy
for what he was always about to say: *to the moon, Alice!*
in the dingy quarters

by the sea of human toil and information we called
The Honeymooners
on television in the fifties.

But why did we think it was so funny?
Alice was his wife and lover, and though it is hard, admittedly,
to picture their lovemaking—
the sweat he heaved into her with a fat man's
slog and fury, not

grace, don't call it grace,

until their headboard,
scrolled with grapes and angels in the old manner,
must have quaked like rails underground, years like that,
layered in concrete, deep,
absorbing the shock and just taking it
because someone said
Cleave Unto Him
and she cleaved, O she cleaved,
smirking—

I can't help it. I do.
Now my Sanitation-working neighbor with a
wife and kid and back rent hanging over their collective heads
like the ghost of Christmas future

fights solidly, drunkenly this week
for two impressive hours,

at the end of which time
they spill onto the matrimonial sidewalk,

dishing it out like this for love:

Leave goddamn you.
Leave.
Just take the baby seat and go. Leave.
I'm not your psychiatrist,
I can't help you with your problems and I'm sick
and you're sick
and I'm sick of you. Meanwhile

nothing in this scene is unequivocal.
The wife weeps and curses, throwing sucker punches.
The baby on the lawn
weeps and howls,
butting his head against a geranium.
And the baby's car seat, for god's sake,

lofted like the very torch of liberty itself
in the husband's arms,
to light the trees—then all of Bakman Avenue if he could.
A mighty conflagration to end
and start things
over again,

back before the high school prom ball spins too many mirrors
over their dopey, lovestruck heads;

before their nosey neighbor
(a stock character in these situation comedies)
puts her finger to the dial
and calls the cops.

❖

Wait. Let me start again.
My father was a sociologist.
My mother a housewife stranded in the desert
without a canteen
if you take my meaning—

five babies in eleven years, very little money.

Not that happiness didn't exist for us sometimes
the way it did for the Petries
in black and white,
                                        Rob, Laura, their son,
Little-Pretty-What's-His-Name. No,
we had our moments,

our birthday parties and bocci on the lawn.
Our trip to Disneyland.
Our trip to Gettysburg.

But when Laura (Rob's due
home any minute. Quick, Milly, help . . .)
gave rise to a self-inflating life raft, huge, forbidden to her
    in her front hall closet
in New Rochelle,
in a place that was also a time and a lack, a pressing need,

we called it an *episode.*
We knew for her there would be
no real rancor,
and no fists raised

beyond the sweet vulgarity of working things out for laughs
until next week
on TV.

❖

Or never.
Look, it's no one's fault; I can buy that.
Our noses flagged,
we were neither charming nor photogenic by the 1970s—
my prolix, super-unsubtle American family
pushing against itself like a live birth in the canal, cramped, uncertain,

angry, dropping down and down without a camera crew
or a script in sight.
What did Walter Cronkite say
when the war I grew up with
ended?
No end at the light of the tunnel?

Something like that.
And there wasn't a light or a life raft for years.

No wonder we'd long since
grown bored with television.
Petulant or high on sleazy
Moroccan hash, my brothers and I had spun from sitcom to soap opera,

from game show host to moon shot
to assassination
and back again, but O the moon shots!
Those men weren't heros; they were straight-arrow, uxorious types,
frolicking in their magic lunar vehicles
as though at some deluxe
country club—segregated, of course.
No wives or children allowed! And in that context

doesn't playing golf up there
make a lot of sense?

Low gravity, high density:

no need to plant our flag too deeply. Who'd want
to claim such a creepy place?
Let alone kill to breathe there.

And the golf ball
hung like a word yet unspoken
for how many years?

❖

Don't look at me like that.
Violence, I have asked myself these questions
as a member of what family, what country,
what honor of blood to blame it on?

My father was a sociologist,
my mother an *agent provacateur* with a nervous habit of M & M peanuts
and staying up late all hours
in her splendid isolation,
for the purpose of taking notes, i.e., What
Jack Parr said.
Why Ed McMahon's teeth looked better
when he was wearing plaids,
why a certain starlet seemed despondent. Personally,

I was sleeping
vouchsafed in the heart of it all,
more abstract than any sleeping child.
Twenty-five years later,
I still can't find my face
in these two-way mirrors I've watched
like a burned out, brainlocked Saint Teresa, waiting for a sign.

❖

Here's a scene
from a movie I never saw on the all night
cable movie classics station:

Barbara Stanwyck
learning she's been framed, or at least suspicious,

reaches for a hankie but this time
gets a good idea, a hand grenade! instead. Catch this, she says.
America,
don't look at me like that.
The dust may never settle.

Still Life with Hummingbird and Typewriter

From a twin flame is born,
out of the White Ovoid is born

the fallen angels' rebellion,
and star people, too, are caught in the karmic wheel

because of fluoride in the water.
Such were the wonders I heard

on Public Access Cable TV
midday

as the sun roasted the neighboring fields
to a tougher nature

under dirt,
and I took a break from writing.

We're all going to seed! Only my cat, Spike, is
working herself down to calico butter

chasing a hummingbird
she's introduced into my room,

dictating the removal of screens and waiting.
Wing-birds, my three-year-old stepson calls them.

Wing-bird,
as though he knew already

the answer to these questions that keep thrumming me:
Is nature subordinate to spirit?

Are you the unmet friend?
The unseen is all around us but today

the sun at meridian
reveals what I need to know of the magic

and dread of each day,
the terrible want of data on our faces

made plain. I love you, I've blurted out
more than once to a stranger, then

whistle, whistle,
don't mind me,

I'm just like ol' Walt here,
out of the cradle nervously talking. Get it? Elbow

in the ribs.
Get it? Get it?

Oh love, the men at the JoyPlex this afternoon
watching smutty movies

imagine the dream come of a thousand
sexual choices;

they have nothing on us.
Nor do the producers of policies

at the Great and Standard Life Insurance Company,
where ghostly numbers sprout like mushrooms

after rain
(as if we didn't know)

to tell us what we're worth.
Nor the woman downtown who mixes a home brew of Lysol and bleach

in her basement to induce
abortion—she's a florist by trade. She's tired,

she can't do this again.
Nor the law clerks, the factotums, the kiss-asses,

the argus-eyed,
the Franciscans with their lovely dinnerware, the all night

pizza delivery boy, the sales clerks, the mobile
dog groomers, the bookies, and bread makers

and journeymen
Sheetrock finishers walking on stilts

to reach up into the high corners where no one sees us
but God and the spiders

who aren't, at any rate, saying
how exactly we *will* outwait them all

in the necessary restless
waiting department of our days, and live, just live.

Because a hummingbird has landed, pursued,
on my typewriter today,

my space bar, my daft
daisy wheel,

take the door off the hinges.
Darken those openings which appear

to be exits,
but are not. Spike,

many more things are possible. You with your infinite pity,
me with feathers in my mouth,

minutes sound their infinitesimal
engines in the ear

and who would have guessed it? A tiny
bird like a bloody tooth, our terrified,

cowering savior.
In the gaps, too, there is matter, matter, matter.

Shirts & Skins

Last year my neighbor's son,
an ordinary beautiful boy of fifteen or sixteen,
began falling *for no reason,* as we like to say.
For months he measured a staircase
by the bruises under his skin,
the yellow sunsets there.
A high curb
might mean damage outright.

Surely this was disease
as we fear it most,
the blank waters rising around his ankles, unnaming him.
And the doctors?
They were tourists in a ghost town he'd left behind
without marks or maps, no calling out.

They washed their clean hands of him.
He was alone then
in a calmer body.
He was deep space before stars and planets

come whistling fire through,
throwing open their tin-edged windows.

❖

Now imagine this,
a cure strong as change and unexpected
as the absence of regret.
Later that year, when the killer browns and blue-reds
had come back to the leaves
as if, this time,

they'd never go away,
he was again driving and feinting downcourt
behind the vacant Sons of Italy.

What I remember most was his nonchalance.
He shot from the top of the key
hours the day he was released,
shrugging the ball up, and
running with a strong limp like a man
whose feet had already accepted
two different earths, fair and unfair.

The ragged playground's net
blowing by a thread.

❖

Who knows what pulls us up and saves us
from ourselves, or from God-who-loves-us,
or for how long?

Watching my neighbor's son,
I thought of how many times my own legs
had been returned to me,
real after weeks or days of numb, shuffling sadness.
A perfect succession of days marked
either by self-pity, or fear, or both, not to mention
the little dooms,
the hundred hairbrained schemes my heart is given to,
so that it would seem
I'd knee-walked home from an all night gin party
in a morgue

or a fraternity house: weeping drunk,
too full of my sad wonderfulness. Then waking,

not to the old sadness or happiness, but to a condition
I recognize chiefly
for its dependable qualities.
Like the president of the high school mathematics club who waited

a hundred mornings for me
on my parents' front porch,
with yellow leaves stuck to the soles of his Weejuns
and his cowlick at attention.

He was ready to walk me back to class
if I would only say the word.

We live by displacement,
by wish and what really comes.
The day my neighbor's son was released,
the dark got worse right on schedule;
it wiped down a russet sky
where the toothless oaks, the blue
boxhedges leaned in.

I remember thinking, what's the point in prognosis?

In the hour of faith and revision,
in late afternoon when nothing is safe,
everything makes
a kind of sense.
A woman, feeling only slightly theatrical,
lifts her head from crossed arms

where she rests at the kitchen table
because she sees it now—
how everything worked out for the best.

And a boy with one leg shorter than the other
goes up against the moon,
rebounding then testing his vertical strength
until night swings down,
double-jointed,
from the monkey bars of the trees, and grabbing hold,
sets him casually free.

Vanity Fair

—Nureyev, AIDS, 1993

We are sick with the news.
Too beautiful, too elegant, refined—too young—
the body in question
self-whittled,
so that we see in the grim business of this contagion

its doubling,
the lovely living face
displaced by skull beneath it as though
eaten out by dreams, or by an old
outcropping of stone, ontologically forced. A comedy, really:

A boy treks the Urals with a pair of toe shoes
hung around his neck like satin counterweights
of charm and lethal luck.
Handhold over reach,
he does not fall until he chooses to fall

beautifully, impeccably,
into the stricken gendarme's arms in 1961,
seeking asylum.
Then the grand jeté, protracted,
onto the pages of every well-heeled society rag

and rotogravure,
a sly Mercury grinning sidelong in red suede
over-the-knee boots and Greek fisherman's cap—
gravity did not know his name.
Neither humility. Who cared? He flew with clarity, the kind

that ties our hearts' first cause
to the fates of those we love and cannot know.
Too rich, out of reach: Lee Radziwill.
Then there is the matter of records
he broke and set.
Eighty-nine curtain calls with Dame Fonteyn as Sleeping Beauty

meant he had to sit in floribunda roses,
waist deep, to wait the cheering out.
Princely pancake makeup sweating off.
We know the rest.
In *Vanity Fair* the last photos went unretouched.
His eyes, bulging, recalled a thoroughbred's in the moments

before the barn goes up,
knotted breath and starveling look,
then ten years in the burning.
Fifty, for all we know.
And no maxims of dignity, or talent's "hard, pure flame"

can change this fact.
No pearl-lined casket driven hand over hand along
gold balustrades of the Paris Opera House
can tear the truth asunder
to which we are wedded now.

La Bayadere, Le Corsaire, half of Broadway's
queer kick line, Keith Haring,
sweet Willi Smith.
Against our wills we register another name
dimming out among the distant addresses of stars.
Those of us who survive aren't dancing,

we're barely keeping up.
Now, when we read of art in magazines complete with ads
perfumed beyond enduring,
rot of roses—tear them out!—we pause,
and stare past our yard
to the neighbor's, whose ridiculous Chow has papers

drawing his royal dog line
from ancient cities of China buried like so much
chipped dinnerware,
so many fossilized soup bones and femurs.
And our gins and tonics
in a cold sweat,

the wind flipping pages at random, indiscriminately,
pages our fingers have damped
and marred with the magic oils of our hands—
it is, finally,
the banal horror of it all

we cannot seem to name.
Now a magazine must be held in our laps
as a gravestone and a portable grave.
We can take it with us everywhere.
Still, it drives us inward to a never vanishing

point of hope read with despair
we cannot meet or transcend.
Transcend? Art for art's sake is dead at last,
the word's in.
We are not misty souls in a vale of our own
making and rare,

but are human, flummoxed, reminded, numb.
Contagion, too, is grounded in this: someone's been had.
The Chow wheezes, scratches
for a blood-fat tick.
There are no gods in *Vanity Fair*.

On First Looking Into Wells Fargo and Seeing a Rock Star

The teller is uncanny,
one minute flying around with her head off
like Nike of Samothrace, wings hyperextended—
more penny rolls!—

the next she is a candlelit room,
her face an Easter lily. Even the security guard
sucks in his gut.
He won't be calling the district manager a needle dick today.

He won't be eating
just any cold sandwich.
And the Mistress of Loans?
She's grown expansive, plumb, well dressed.

In the presence of rock's handsome superindifference,
she's a punk explorer
expert at the gilded vault's
big wheel; she wants, it's clear, to take us someplace

from somewhere we've never been.
She wants to give us some.
But we are shy.
We bow our heads. We bob like poor swan boats

washed up in the old accounts line,
despite word coming in from Dublin and Detroit
that our grim business will be graced,
our debts canceled into shining

if we can only stop grinning, and look at your,
look at your . . .
O sex and sex and magnificent refusals!
As you make your way from record cover to restaurants

strung a thousand ways with ravishing
actressy smiles,
before you think to roust the corner deli for Jack Daniels and Sudafed,
and are borne by limousine

well past our best days'
roaring tedium,
stay a while with the rest of us.
We hold the suspicion you live the life

on which our vindications lie.
Stay. One brief transaction, one cosmic
zap of a glance connects us
over the top of your blue granny glasses.

It might be all it takes
to reinvent ourselves backwards from your fine raggedness.
Then we are not wrong in school, sad
pimply woebegones.

We are not bland martinets at work
though our bosses smile & stab.
Our wives don't cheat, our husbands never bald.
Our children revere us.

They think we are cool.
We *are* cool—cooler than ever thought possible.
Even in the womb we were so.
Cool fetuses, zygotes, womb

trinkets, treasure,
planned for,
loved beyond all customary reasons for being loved in this world.
And the mother who carried us for ourselves alone

was cool, who poured the mother syrup
over us, cooing to the inside.
Who did not sip port wine all day dreading
something not knowing what,

though she held the spitting steam iron up between herself
and the television's partial eclipse,
Edge of Night,
and stalled, thinking to melt the screen.

Likewise our fathers understood their lives.
To the belly they whispered as to a prayer mound.
We swam in the jewelled
aquarium of that sound;

we rocked our boats in the same slipstream. Imagine,
to be only just conceived
and rich. The man, spent, blissed, rolls off.
The woman closes her eyes because it seems to her

that she has just raised a chalice
and an old box microphone to her lips.
Sliced clarity of violin strings and the blue moon rising to sing
its dust in her hair, dust and notes,

gardenias, hush,
clink of glasses, desire town, *play it, brother,*
a goddamned fool—
she will not be that again.

The Vinegarroon

Once, out walking the low pass between two hills
of no particular beauty
save they were there, like the couple,
half green,
breathing dust,
blind to the other faces they wore
in the other resonant valleys below,

and the crows' unhinged articulations
ringing out, the first stars
invisible, for this was a summer evening and light,
bearing invisible witness to—what,
pure seeing?—

they saw a vinegarroon,
plated in its bright coppery
sectioned shell
with whip-tail joints all business, pincers
vised on a baby tarantula
it was dragging across the road.

Taken together,
spider and scorpion,
the scene was fantastic, a brooch one's grandmother
might have worn in the thirties
with rhinestones for eyes.
Imagine a keepsake tarantula,
a prize catch for dinner
and may the best venom win!

The man and woman shuddered. Ahead
lay chaparral and sky
nicked here and there by clouds.
Behind them, the sounds of the party they'd left to be alone

and unobserved
rose on the wind like uncertain mantras;
separate voices were indistinguishable
even as the air disclosed them,

though someone might have said *pesto,*
another *sabbatical,* or *ruin.*
The music was vintage Sinatra.

"Once," the man said slowly, enunciating, circumspect, not mean
but not yielding, either,
rubbing wild sage
between his palms for effect,

"once I put the bones of some leftover childhood dinner—
chicken paprikash, I think—
into a jar of cider vinegar and waited two weeks.
When they were done steeping,

I brought them out and amazed my chums—
they were rubber bones then. Bendable
as the joke chickens they used to use in vaudeville
to whack a gullible
fellow over the head,
but more stripped down, of course,
and to the point.
Post–post-modern, I guess you'd want to call them.
Though this was before your time."

Now this is how the young woman came to feel like crying.
Understand she had trusted him
as any good grad student would trust her best professor,
and he a married anthropologist with tenure!
She watched his fingers grow

lightly stained with green; the knuckles
ground a little.
Fingers that had raised

her clit in pleasure:
the smell of sage was everywhere, clean heaven.
The vinegarroon, when she remembered to look for him, was gone.

The walk back was uneventful. No one had missed them.
In fact, during the dissolution
of this love affair,
the party had grown gayer.
Smart women wearing expensive, idiosyncratic jewelry,
sat on antique milking stools,
smiling as their men recounted
oral exams
which might have been taken yesterday,

so fresh was their terror.
Tipsy, the host with great magnanimous gestures
fed the giant koi he kept
in a stone pond where the newly risen moon
had just begun to writhe
and settle
and calcify.
The fish jumped for every magic bite. These pellets

that kept them spangly and false
made their orange tails
work the water to a boil.
And dinner? That was a late matter of some artichokes,
a sauce for dipping,
and some well-built steaks.
Sour cream for potatoes, baked, and chives, alfresco;
you get the point,

until each in turn had scraped the green petals down
with his or her sharp teeth, sipped
some Pinot Noir
to stiffen the backbone, the long
drive home with one's long-suffering spouse . . .

I knew a guy once, who,
a young professor started, then looked out
beyond her plate and laughed
and shook her head.
Last March she'd tried to kill herself
with a Swiss army knife.
Victorinox.

Nobody dared move or chew. No one said a word.
Then, as sometimes happens
here on earth, the moonlight
grew amazingly, idiotically bright,

like a loutish man with a metal plate in his head,
who after the accident keeps asserting
it's stainless steel,
and go ahead,
go ahead and hit him.
These things happen. It never was your fault.

Then a phone rang twice inside and stopped.
A pair of brown bats,
stirred by whatever instincts drive
so fluttering an engine,
dove one after the other for the speck
of a crumb of an insect

smaller than a mote in the eye.
Then Sinatra came and went again, feelingly.
Then the embarrassed laughter that swims, feckless,
up to the surface, and relief,
signaling the end of the meal.

The Nude Detective, a Complaint

—for God

Your devices are sensitive.

In rain and in snow,
in moonlight that clatters down

its bright plates and crockery
like a voice in the head,

you stay. You lend to our windows
a fishing pole

and a microphone.
But why?

Are you some under-assistant's
last hireling?

Nothing, not even faith or crazy envy explains
how we provoke you to this patience

hour by hour.
And if our daily static can be removed,

our *yeses*
turned to *no* on tape

the way technology puts
plastic hearts in men, or

cheese in jars,
then surely we don't deserve

such a careful listening.
Such bare attention to what we do

only makes us act worse.
A kiss, a gasp—

how long before you drag
your sunburned knuckles in some fleshly

circles on the ground?
How long before you order moo shu pork then drip

plum sauce on the bedsheets?
Mr. Never Kissed and Tell, Mr.

Truly Exposed,
we're speaking out at last.

You wearing just a porkpie hat
like Donatello's *David*,

you with dark circles under wholly
permanent eyes, we wish you'd get a life

and beat it for good this time, you goddamn,
you shivering

angel who loves us more than we love ourselves.

Vivid Video

On a radio somewhere a French boy is rapping
about his *coeur bleu.*
It's blue, it seems, for some
not so obvious reasons—the will to be contained
in me, in you, in anyone.
"Dig in anyone's shadow, you find
a turning grave,"
Muriel Rukeyser said.
With my bleared eyesight, a dozen
roots of sleeplessness in my hands, mug of hot milk,

I offer this up to you:
the indecent riff of my neighbor's lovemaking at 4 A.M.
comes complete with abrading thighs,
antiphonal structures,
groans—*groans*—and the caterwaul and great
promise of red roses. And furthermore,
and furthermore,
I sputter, I fume.
I have to work tomorrow! Oh,

heavy destiny,
to live above Sophia Samantha, porn babe
extraordinare, who aspires
in her own middle class way
by acting for a living, and who now in off hours
works also for a spring wardrobe
and a weekend on Catalina.

Have you heard this before?
That people in drycleaned clothes begin absorbing—
each hour of each workday,

head down over figures, quotes, *I'll*
get back to you Sal after I buzz
my jobber in Buffalo, great guy, he took me
flyfishing I stepped once
on a rainbow by mistake, bit my foot to the bone,
those gills, I can't
wear my Florsheims anymore, squish, squish—

cleaning fluid. And so
they begin their lifelong death in suits they've worn
like a river and a floating home.
Like being embalmed
from the outside in.
Vivid Video.
It helps me to think about the film company
this way: paper clips.
What kind do they use? Traditional silver,
or the pastel, vinyl-coated kind?
All things being equal, shots

framed and the books in need of balancing,
is there a dental plan
that makes sense?
Mafia ties?
Is a hole as good as a slit if we're talking
holes and slits—and why not?—
in Saturnalian repose around a jug of wine,
a studded belt
(extension cords will do),
a jar of Vaseline, and a hot tub steaming its late
liberation theology? Christ!

❖

Some nights, when I'm awakened like this
by a sound I cannot bear plainly,
then do, I'm alone.
I sense I'm missing someone, but who is it?
My bone blonde neighbor, her shrill
pipistrelle cries
zigzag into my hair;
they stir me down improbably
toward three more good hours of sleep.

Other nights, I'm tuned to my pillow's
highest frequency, warden
of what's not right.
Jump started and sleep deprived,
hammer hearted,
I'm no grunge princess—who do they think they are?
And Samantha Sofia will not know me anyway
in the parking lot by the pool
where she floats unstrapped
for hours, comatose,
cucumber slices for eyes.

She will not know me on the stairway
juggling groceries until Minute Rice comes raining
like a wedding through the hole.
Nor will she suffer my automatic pity
for her chosen field,
this soft and hard auto-autobiography.
Vivid Video,

tonight my head is closed for business,
my face is heart-shaped,

my hands wide open.
If a French boy is singing on a radio somewhere
about his blue heart, it's because
there's a hole in it I can't discern or fill,
corresponding to the holes in the microphone
of the lady on the 24-hour cable shopping channel

preaching Tonal Dressing with Accessories, including,
but not limited to,
rhinestone appliqués, scarves, straw hats, hair
bands and hair scrunchees, alligator belts, liquid
silver jewelry, and a really good
leather clutch.

Believe it or not, I understand
the importance of all this.
In 1965, in the ancient year of 2 A.Z.—
two years after Zapruder's film caught the president's face
low, imploding into light—
my sister, Ellen, would craze and bawl and jab
when I stole her first lipsticks
and smeared myself
frosted pink.
She was sinking already then, having no good role model
for angry, democratic womanhood;

she hurled hairbrushes at me instead.
But I was glamorous at last!
And what, the world was never the same after that?
We're all born famous,
then frame by frame
we grow less so, lucky in the end if anyone listens to us

or knows our real name.
Mine is Dorothy. I'm banging

on the floor with a hand that's mine—
it's still covered in flesh—
which is how I know
I haven't sunk too far in sorrow or desire
or disappeared yet.
Shut up! Shut up!

From the apartment below, muffled laughter, not unkind,
then the sound of water running
down very old drains.
My mother used to hold out a warm towel to me
after I'd bathed.
I remember searching that blanked, assiduous face,
and a voice saying, though her lips never moved,
we'll all be dead tired on the job tomorrow.

On the Poisoning of a Neighborhood Cat

Glitter of April in southern California, faithful morning,
the sky has pronounced itself

perfectly blue.
Sunlight pours from bougainvillea to vetch.

And who has been discomforted today?
Who has found it hard, no, impossible,

to live a moment longer
in a world of woes unceasing,

small as paw prints muddying an Audi
or a Corolla, freshly washed? A saucer of antifreeze

might be placed, well, anywhere—near that tire iron there,
or this canvas lawn chair

unstrapped for the season.
We are human beyond imagination in most matters.

But what to do until the county comes
with its valid truck, measure of swift and absolute removal?

From nearby apartment buildings a few
neighbors have gathered on the blonding grass.

Four years lack of rainwater
hasn't killed it yet. There's low talk of that, nervous, then

of hearty strains and the undisputed
wisdom of "drought-resistant planting."

Then nothing. As St. John and the City of Los Angeles
claim, the body shall be raised

incorruptible.
Until then, let the left eye be forced

slightly from the round earth of its socket, haywire vision,
and a pencil line of blood

be drawn from each shell pink ear into the dust.
Let this sack of fur be compounded

into limp desires now.
With each fair breeze the hills above Glendale

and Pasadena, and Eagle Rock,
threaten to shake loose

the pollen that begins a crazy explosion here,
with lushness of leaves, seeds

bolting back, and oleander, oleander,
not a raincloud in sight.

It's almost magic. Not like making the proverbial rabbit
appear—that's always been our strength.

More, making him look so damned startled each time
the hat clamps down around him again

like a pot lid.
Jackhammer, our hearts, what we are afraid of in ourselves

cannot be recorded sufficiently.
There isn't enough time.

Ants begin taking their capable place
in the breakdown of things as they are.

Neighbors move on.
Paws draw up mildly in full sun.

Noah Descending

Noah, in the dream of Swirl Down and Swim Away
which is not your fate,
your arms stretch long
and fine as filament moonlight. In reality,

the wine hits home.
Blind staggers on the rough boards and coiled
rope snakes on deck.
The shovel for mucking out stalls falls over;
it sings a drinking song as it goes: "There once was a girl
from Nantucket . . . "

You act disgraceful.
With your excellent high weeping
you wake the family.

But it is not your fate to say no.
Life as it was is a hat on the ocean, floating away from you.
Or is that Mount Ararat
showing through fog its puny,
unadvertised peak?
And how far, Noah? Where?
God's word goes and goes.

God's bearings will not budge.
Face it as you would the navigable stars
if there were any to see.
Now sleep it off,
snoring, bathetic,
right here in the new world's new inclemency,

while your family settles
again in this ship's true hold: dreaming.
The Big Heads of Nervous
Animals Dream.

The Green Gauze Lifting Dream.
You dream, too, of drowned towns you'll visit someday

as the unsmiling
undersecretary of choice and apparent choice,
where palm trees and a few mad
villagers pinned by rocks
understand.

With the action of waves their arms lift and lower, slowly,
to shake hands with you as you pass.
And the great stone
lantern fish of the moon,
lit under pressure,
its one eye-stalk will not swerve.
It leads you further on.

Crow Sermon

—et lux in tenebris lucet

Do not be a fool; if you must be one,
avoid wearing plaid.
Eat half of all the food given you
over your lifetime.
Defecate quietly.
Do not be the sum of your history.
Do not stand under the candy-cane
caduceus of the barber pole
imagining your soulmate will happen by
just because you have the right sideburns.
We all wait.
We all burn.
Poverty our parent, loneliness, regrets,
what makes you think we need to add
your puny hoo-ha to this list?
Believe me, from up here on the wires
your head resembles
a cactus apple; in the dark,
old women sit crocheting
cobwebs for your funeral.
Don't cry.
Verily I say to you
I'm a new kind of old style god: partly
an asshole, like you, and partly sweet
and so damned earnest
it could make ten cherubs
weep for pride.
Me, I never cry.
I sky by sky, shrieking my raw
capitulations to human industry.
"There," I say,

"is a loiterer," "There a woman
wearing the larval membrane
of a miniskirt, soliciting."
Cops and politicians love me.
The lathe of my black wings
turns to fashion: me!
flying at truly impressive heights.
Do you think I'm pretty?
I'm Jesus' thirteenth disciple,
Doubtful Promise, and in some
important ways
I know you to be the kind of person
a bird like me can trust,
reduced as you are.
Hold out your hand.
I've got some magic corn
and this stuff, eaten,
is guaranteed to transform you into a princess,
even if you're a man. Who cares?
The ruby tiara fits. Servants scrape.
It's what you've always wanted,
vast entitlement.
Of course, I've lately been eating
some Mission figs, whose drawstring purses
pucker to a ripe
red meat and seeds in a lather, and it's, well,
messy business,
this distribution and dropping of
your upward mobility.
Forgive me.
With my rasp and my caw
and my sawtooth wings and my sweet
mother lode,

I'm what you've prayed for and prayer
really is simple.
Ask and it shall be given;
details to be worked out later.
Good. I like the way you've taken to your knees
(prostration is sometimes
a lovely touch)
to praise me.
We make a handsome pair, don't you think?
You with your arms out in a bent
axis of shaking relief,
me with my deadeye cruising,
cruising—now! Look up.
Once more shall cool gods and
wretched men
make their steady progress
toward a fixed position,
heaven.

Surfing as Meditation

Sex Wax, the best wax for your stick!
—motto for a national brand of surfboard wax

On Sunday,
all the dry hours listening to Pastor Kywitt explain
why man is so sad
in the twentieth century.
                                        Don't ask, he says.
Then he tells them anyway.

Drinking and dancing.
Smoking. The shadowing forth of women's ways. He says
we are starvelings bidden by a percolating lust
and considerable sin,
affliction, yea Lord, affliction.

He says REPUDIATE.
He says PREVAIL.
But a day like this rinsed of meaning, two hours
served by joy—

a thin stretch of whale's road
is nothing to a sad young man!

So the boy is rollicked along
in a parrot green wetsuit, alien and raised up,
the curtain rent or else
the dark divisible by his blonde hair alone,
and if pastor's God can't be satisfied
ever, amen,
then knowing that helps.

Knowing it starts as one thing and ends as another, in waves.
And I am not who I was, he says.
I am not who I was

as he paddles out again dripping,
moderatissimo,
leveling long arms into the water's stiff harangue.
But what about shorebreak?
White water signals a change;

currents go funny
and that's all she wrote—
apocalypso millennium.

Just like that you're washed out to sea
with a leash around your ankle
and the sharks
thick as Catholic soup on Fridays. Catholic-school girls
everywhere! Temptation

is hardly irrelevant.
In these hard-pressed, Foursquare, teenage years,
sunset pounds the water still
as mirrored planks.
His heart expands promiscuously
to let it all in: the day and the toweling off,

scritch scratch of sand,
his erection
pulling a little as he crouches down as he catches

his breath to name one passion
we're not punished for.
You think *these* are waves?
You say balance like this comes easily, like walking
on the tossing manes of lions
or blue, blue wheat?

In the one true theocracy,
only he who prays himself black & blue will be saved, sucked,
embodied,
all the way to Zuma Beach and beyond
in one glorious undertow of spirit over choice,
because there is no choice—
if it's true.

Fuck the body! the body!
cry the bitterns and red-eyed gulls
diving for their dinner. Like us,
they'd sooner crash some days than burn for a fish.

But one morning a wetsuit
left waving on the line,
animus-empty,
on a porch lit with raspberry bougainvillea blooming,
reminds us of someone who got away
just in time, who skipped town with his open secret
like a precious wound,
naked, before a mob of the converted
descended with their sticks.

—for Phil

Icarus Holds the Trouble Light

—for my father and my brothers

1. The Boss Hog Himself

Have you noticed how fathers grow deadly
in the duty zone?
Whose fault is that?
Whose idea among all the ideas
that ride this world,
that in nearly every home a vampire lives
all night caffeined
to the supernal chant of *fix it, fix it*

only he hears?
When he protests, "This job is killing me!"
to the sprung toasters
and caulk oozing from squeeze guns
and nails rusting to tetanus, ruffed with a wicked orange fur,

the father gets bigger, strong as blood on this diet,
while the sour son he's recruited to help him
shrinks, fades, oxygen poor.

2. The Trouble Light

One of those caged affairs.
A cross between a pirate hook and a flashlight, industrial strength,
to have and to hold or hang
in basements and garages, rank
cave places, primordial, stuck,
tar pits of do-it-yourself and joint compound,
girlies on girlie calendars grinding

their teeth into their lips, smiling, bending over,
glue, in pots, sapped from horses hooves, and metal on metal—
that smell—
and every broken part, and men.

3. The Tool Virgin

There are spirits in a bottle of paint thinner; the label
tells us so. It's perfectly natural,
something soft inside the hard thing
that keeps stripping us bare.
So, too, a deep function of fatherhood to work on junk cars
whilst lecturing the son who most disappoints you
because he *is* you, sooner or later:

"Like this and like this and like this," Daddy says,
Daddy's name in this case being Daedalus.
"Like this and like this and like this.
Now hold the light still
so I can see to build a sweat, grease the works,
consult the sky for oracular Slant-6 maintenance tips."

Daedalus is on a roll!
On the wheeled dolly, on his back, he rides like vintage sex
the raised machine.
He's putting the rend into rendered.
He's taking the dead out of Daedalus.
And Icarus? He's a tool virgin.
He's too young to touch these tools.
He's not allowed to try the interesting stuff. His job

is to hold and hold.
Hold until his arms quake, they shiver,

and the trouble light with its murderous, mindful,
one-eyed glow grows
hot, heavy,
pitching forward the one who always
manages to slip up, somehow—
"Goddammit boy! How many times . . . "

4. Now

Now from up and down their street
lamplight begins to burnish shades.
Lamps set close to windows are being turned on
one cricket's worth of click, click
at a time. 5:30 P.M., a veritable
domestic symphony, poor as it is.
Mothers set creamed corn on the table.
Husbands cough lung in the next room, distracted, dreaming that upstairs
their sons stand at attention, waiting
for their fathers to become children in diapers again,

wheeled around, gumming for
one last good idea,
because we will not understand in time
the nature of our refusals.

5. Daedalus Softens, Thinking of Beer

He fixes to repair for a cold one soon.
He ruffles Icarus' hair.
"Shit, kid. Help me a little longer,
and I'll let you take this baby for a spin around the neighborhood.
A good steep grade, speed, no
guardrails, really let her out, fly and

come back and tell me
if this brake job holds."

Wrong Icarus grins derelict freedom, grins
as though he were wearing feathered underwear! Dreams, unfathered,
he puts his arms down for good.

The Older Brothers of Girls I Grew Up With

did not have names, and those names keep playing my memory:
Deracinated. Obstinate. Born To Be High. White Enough. Scary Movie.
Transparent Membrane. Me But Better.

The older brothers of girls I grew up with
did not go to triple canopy jungles to die—they weren't old enough
and never would be—but went home from class instead

to walnut-paneled family rooms presided over by one beer sign,
and ignominious cocktail napkins, and dry, mixed nuts.
There the principalities of stain on the sculptured carpet

meant something; they could figure it out.
They had that much time, and a terrible patience, and no
gratitude to speak of. Their philosophy in fact was to smoke time
whole

by taking it into the yellow lungs directly, then holding it
until even the one-armed DJ spinning late nights at WMMS
sputtered and grew teary-eyed,

and the calendar stalled, and one by one those nights and days fell
off the page
coughing, twisting their ankles,
and someone had to slap just about everyone's back and yell,

breathe, dammit. Just let it go.
The older brothers of girls I grew up with did not have jobs,
though they "handled baggage," or "caddied," or "bussed tables" in
hairnets

in restaurants whose kitchens stunk of French dressing and
minimum wage.
They did not date. Back then a girlfriend made house calls.
Closing the bedroom door,

she'd take the toot from his smeared mirror, put
the boy's hand on her breast, manipulate the nipple herself,
ride the bump in his pants, a dry fuck. Then she'd do the guy's
 homework!

It was, I don't know,
the seventies, you know?
A chocolate bar could extend the life of a starving child by eleven
 days—

the real soldiers knew that. But they were dead or gone or draining
shit and tears down the Mekong Delta. Bivouacked
beyond the beyond, while the older brothers of girls I grew up with

had only the memory of red deer crossing
the flannel lining of Boy Scout sleeping bags, on camping trips they
 took
back when their penises were feathered things,

and their hands golden pheasant, ring-necked, calling home.
Did I mention Janis Joplin in those smoky unfamous family rooms
scalding us with "Piece of My Heart,"

boning us like white fish flopped out of our skins,
her voice the only good sex most of us would know for years?
 Furthermore,
there were no parents around,

and a brown plaid sofa completed the scene.
But I'm no photojournalist; I had a place and a stake in this, too.
I won the rights to a long line of idiot witnessing

because I was a girl, thirteen, waiting under the zero gaze
of American cool for the one bad line of credit
I could call my own. Someone to lay down my life for.

Once, one of the brothers spoke to me and made
all my waiting worthwhile. Unstuck! I would not die doddering and
alone
in a singed, unseemly world. It was March or February.

We lived near Cleveland International Airport,
where the DC-10's took off every hour into long gaps of gray skies,
spew of refineries, oil barge lights, heavy-

head weather we called it, the concussion of take-off
like something of human importance
though we'd grown immune to the sound. And the brother asked,
softly,

examining his cracked hands,
"Dorothy, do you know what ringworm looks like?"
I don't know what I said, but I remember the extravagance with which

I blushed, the stone milk of kindness opening my veins,
my heart leaking joy as though I'd eaten meat from the moon.
Who says we live without purpose

though selfish to the core? It's a free country!
War isn't the worst thing to happen to a boy and girl.
And I vowed then I'd go forward with love and awe
to tell our stupid tale.

The Prodigal Daughter

If a daughter bent on pleasing
turns her knives
inward, then the salad plate goes

to the left of the glassware,
the cup aligned
with the soup spoon—where were we? Oh, yes,

the prodigal daughter
did not return.
She never left home in the first place.

And if the fatted lamb is brought to the spit & fire
in her honor,
his black head split jowl to jowl

so that the jewels of his brain
are sizzling, for pudding,
the snout a gourd scooped out

for pomegranate wine,
then she has made that dinner
and that unending drama.

In the gray hierarchy of cook smoke,
let her symbols go up:
ash and amaranth,

the ankle bracelet off at the stump.
This is not the story
of the water in the well,

but of the dutiful woman who might throw herself
down any moment
just to hear the splash,

then refrains. (Refrain)
This is not the new dispensation.
This is not the different earth.

Her old mother is crazy; she's smearing
roast garlic on her cheeks and reading
the riot act to the chickens

with a paring knife.
Her father? He's not gone yet, but he *needs*
her so—who will take care of him

in his early retirement?
Mutiny. Even the least fallen angels
take a dive sometimes. But that

she will not do.
There are dishes to do, and bread
to pound senseless, and dancing classes, and all those

damn sparks to contend with
around the fire pit
clicking its castanets. So what if she caught fire?

What if she who gave herself away so lavishly
in the interest of others
were sent up in a whippet of smoke

to signal the tribes: here is a woman
who was granted the mastery
of one thing, herself,

good-bye!
Outside, the road lays down
its dusty hammer and tongs,

field mice nest in the skulls of wolves,
and worms eat their way toward God
through dirt, or vice versa.

But who is this woman of blank hosannahs,
this genteel, wellborn
woman bound by pity or mercy or self-spite

to spin at the wall, plotting: and who, in any case,
will protect her if she leaves
from all the prodigal sons hitchhiking

like so much unclaimed freight by the side of the road,
sticking out their spoiled thumbs?
They have a lot of living to do

before they settle down
and marry that
cute thing next door, this

dervish in suspense, in tears.
Quick, someone sing a cheery song
about disgrace

and many veils.
Someone count the silverware.

For Andrew, Setting Out on a Long Journey Alone

A stepmother is a made thing;
she can come undone.
At LAX the forced hum of cheerfulness announces
family arrivals, bags checked, navigational charts read
as a dream of life unloosed, and customs,
and the lights of the petrochemical plants
of El Segundo
shining like authorities in the dark.

Your father is nervous, high-strung.
Tonight his boy will be shifted too long
among clouds. A boy could fall from that uncourteous sky.
Passport? Check. Asthma inhaler? Check.
Toys? The kid in the ultra green Ninja Turtle backpack
wants to ride the baggage belt to France! Destroyer

of Legos and Lincoln Logs, wrecker of peace, ring bearer,
brown-eyed like his real mother—
I never had you lodged inside me, explorer.
When we met you were already walking.
You were the perfect diapered miniature of monster ego and beauty
each child is, and by then
it *was* a race; I was off balance

proferring skim milk and faded circus Band-Aids.
Cheered on, I was also exhorted to loosen up.
Underwear? Check.
Through the metal detector we pass single file but
three-headed, as though through a too tight
wedding archway

pledging our electric love of force fields
separate and intact.
Or is this the machinery that zapped the bride of Frankenstein awake

into her lot in life,
which was to be clumsy, stiff-armed, bad with small details—
a supporting player
not a stunt double—
but in the end, big picture-wise, too late?

Soon the Atlantic, towards and away,
will move in its two directions below you,
endlessly turning out its green pockets, though good sleeper,
you'll be unaware of the emptiness
found in that fumbling search. That comforts.
And Veronique waits irrefutably to wake you, *Andrew,*
mon petit lapin, c'est moi!
on the other shore. Dual citizen, like me,

will you insist on answering her in English
then refuse for a full four seconds to grin?
I am no one's mother. You are my son.
This is the truth with my eyes closed: relief,
roar of Paris, this plane is finally taking off.
Myself I accuse of generosity's intermittent radar blips, then
with the part of me that understands these things,
mourn the missing parts.

But on the observation deck
your father pines full on for you.
He sees you again in your hospital incubator, pink as sunrise, flying solo.
I should touch his shoulder, or the place where his hair
breaks in waves, but my hand falters
in the air your parting will always ruin.
Summers and holidays we tremble
along such seams; alone at last, we are divided, unconcluded.
Go, come back soon.
What have you done to me.

Shoestore Monkey

The Owner: forget he's just a boring guy with a shoestore
and a monkey to boot, and he'll
still *be* that guy—that's the thing of it—
with a cage between the Thomas heels
and the double-D wides,
the lifts, the delicate
pantyhose wash.
Orthotics can only do so much, he's been heard to say,
shrugging to heaven because, really,

he'd wanted to sell computers,
and before that, be a cop.
Look at the damage God does, he says,
addressing the bunions.
Little toes like grappling hooks.

Mothers: make no mistake,
this place is great with the kids.
Daily the cage and its monkey receive
the vexed tenderness of families a lot like yours,
glad for any diversion;
to get out of the house for an hour is big.
And if there is no context for loving
a monkey in a shoestore,

it hasn't stopped anyone from feeding it
orange candy peanuts, or taking
its measure with a complimentary
shoehorn—whap, whap.
"Mom, this monkey stinks of monkey poop,"
the older kids shriek, holding their noses.
They like him this way, hanging by his tail,
ignoring them for money.

The Monkey: to him our feet are strange sorrow indeed.
Pale tubors the earth eschews,
barest of bulbs.
It makes him ashamed for us.
It makes him cry out *chi chi,* then *heek heek heek,* like a Marxist
or a pope declaring a new dispensation
that hope is the opposite of hindsight, and home

doesn't hold, and this
the monkey knows: wild chance is truer,
a better bet in the end.
For there is no heart's Serengeti we can count on,
no mountains in China or jungles
in Vietnam, no truly personal computers, no cops
or family relations we understand.
There are no absolute monkeys anywhere, it seems,
except shoestore monkeys, and this is the only one.

Better to sing as he does,
I will not be sad in this world,
presenting his rosebud anus to the bars each time
the cash register rings.
I will not be sad in this world.
See here, you with your excellent credit rating and boxes
tied tidily with string—
don't his fingers on the iron bars
remind you of yours when you were very young? But stronger,
cased in leather.

The Jaws of Life

The Road Ends Here.
That is what the sign says to the ache
and jaw-buzz of jackhammers
pounding Ventura Boulevard
into Coldwater,

but yesterday it ended somewhere else, and tomorrow
somewhere else again,
with a Chevy overturned and a fire hydrant blowing
à la Old Faithful

fifty feet over the heads of the paramedics
who cut into metal with tremendous, fire-tempered hedge trimmers
they'll call the "jaws of life" if you ask them,
so that someone inside
who is trapped
will be free.

❖

With all that water, you'd think
they were fishers of men.

❖

These days a forceps birth
is not recommended.
A baby's skull rides sweeter than a melon
in an eggshell,

those early thumbprints go deeper than anyone feared.
"Connor," my brother said in the odd
wobbly voice of someone

newly overwhelmed by love,
"had a nice little cone,"
from suction the day he was born.

A nice little cone, and would I be the godmother? Which is exactly
the kind of faith it takes these days
to call roads *major arteries,*
or to swim in rivers at night nude, though frankly,
it scares us—
the suddenly cool places, and all
those clear stars beholding us vastly, honking
and beeping their horns,

the bronze temple bell in our chests
ringing as we stroke.

Listen up.
That is what the nuns of the Little Sisters
of Denial used to say
at my old grade school,
doing their best James Cagney.
Here's a story:

For the insurance money a man murders his son, then
has a nervous breakdown.

Later his left arm must be amputated above the elbow
after a freak
lawn mower incident, and he becomes,

now here's the punch line,

psychologically/emotionally healthy again.
Said he'd *suffered enough*
to atone.

❖

As though we really could turn down the volume
on heaven-up-there.

❖

As though rectitude and mercy were just another quiz show
with categories
worth points
depending on the wager, the degree

of difficulty, and how badly
you really wanted it in the first place.

❖

Police Blotter: Roll Call

At approximately 5:48 A.M., Lon and Virginia O'Brien begin making
their tough love next door.
They're rusty, it seems.
Oww, oww—like zapped coyotes they awaken me
because at first I'm thinking
someone is dying, someone is being raped, bludgeoned,
tendon and split lip,
saliva, mud,
so close are the sounds of ecstasy
and expediency,

and although I want to believe pain is not a fit price
for something good in our lives,

there it is again,
that thought in me like a small seizure
overheard through thin walls, with human whirring and weeping,
or the sound a fish makes
as it moves its mouth in purification
over jagged rocks.

Here is how we pray when we are little:
PleaseGodPleaseGodPleaseGodGod.
When we are seasoned, we learn to pray
as once I believed
Protestants do:

Ignore me God,
and I'll ignore you.

We want some assurance, a blanket policy if you will,
that we are not earmarked for exceptional tragedy
or exceptional gain
(which can only lead to tragedy; you see,
I'm Catholic to the end),
and that those we love
will likewise not meet tragic ends.

So far the transaction seems to be working?
The deal holds
as far as it goes.

❖

Yesterday I drove to the pharmacy
to buy some family items.
Vitamin E, my current favorite brand of antiperspirant, fruit-
striped gum for Andrew, batteries, some clear
spermicidal jelly,
which is also tasteless and odorless.
You think life owes you—what? Happiness?
A certain modicum of headache relief?

Starting my car later, I noticed a panhandler
working the parking lot,
wearing a black trash bag for a blouse

—she'd cut where the neck and armholes should be—

and another trash bag for a skirt.
It must have been ninety degrees outside,

and when I rolled down the window to give her
a dollar, which I don't always do
because of logistics, my purse
being vulnerable to robberies and the poor
are with us always,

she looked away. She wouldn't look at me,
but with an odd bobble and fierce craning of her neck,
she compassed the spot where her feet
met burning asphalt, as though to say,
this life and no other!
Neither did she say thank you.
And her toenails were painted bright red.

Dorothy Barresi

Photo: Mary McArthur

lives with her husband, Phil Matero, and sons Andrew and Dante in Los Angeles, California. She is the recipient of fellowships from the Fine Arts Work Center in Provincetown and the North Carolina Arts Council. Her book of poems, *All of the Above*, won the Barnard College New Women Poets Prize. She is associate professor of English at California State University, Northridge.

PITT POETRY SERIES

Ed Ochester, General Editor

Claribel Alegría, *Flowers from the Volcano*
Claribel Alegría, *Woman of the River*
Debra Allbery, *Walking Distance*
Maggie Anderson, *Cold Comfort*
Maggie Anderson, *A Space Filled with Moving*
Dorothy Barresi, *The Post-Rapture Diner*
Jan Beatty, *Mad River*
Robin Becker, *Giacometti's Dog*
Siv Cedering, *Letters from the Floating World*
Lorna Dee Cervantes, *Emplumada*
Robert Coles, *A Festering Sweetness: Poems of American People*
Billy Collins, *The Art of Drowning*
Nancy Vieira Couto, *The Face in the Water*
Jim Daniels, *M-80*
Kate Daniels, *The Niobe Poems*
Kate Daniels, *The White Wave*
Toi Derricotte, *Captivity*
Sharon Doubiago, *South America Mi Hija*
Stuart Dybek, *Brass Knuckles*
Odysseus Elytis, *The Axion Esti*
Jane Flanders, *Timepiece*
Forrest Gander, *Lynchburg*
Richard Garcia, *The Flying Garcias*
Suzanne Gardinier, *The New World*
Gary Gildner, *Blue Like the Heavens: New & Selected Poems*
Elton Glaser, *Color Photographs of the Ruins*
Hunt Hawkins, *The Domestic Life*
Lawrence Joseph, *Curriculum Vitae*
Lawrence Joseph, *Shouting at No One*
Julia Kasdorf, *Sleeping Preacher*
Etheridge Knight, *The Essential Etheridge Knight*
Bill Knott, *Poems, 1963–1988*
Ted Kooser, *One World at a Time*
Ted Kooser, *Sure Signs: New and Selected Poems*
Ted Kooser, *Weather Central*
Larry Levis, *The Widening Spell of the Leaves*
Larry Levis, *Winter Stars*
Larry Levis, *Wrecking Crew*
Walter McDonald, *Counting Survivors*
Irene McKinney, *Six O'Clock Mine Report*
Archibald MacLeish, *The Great American Fourth of July Parade*
Peter Meinke, *Liquid Paper: New and Selected Poems*

Peter Meinke, *Night Watch on the Chesapeake*
Carol Muske, *Applause*
Carol Muske, *Wyndmere*
Leonard Nathan, *Carrying On: New & Selected Poems*
Kathleen Norris, *Little Girls in Church*
Ed Ochester and Peter Oresick, *The Pittsburgh Book of Contemporary American Poetry*
Sharon Olds, *Satan Says*
Gregory Orr, *City of Salt*
Alicia Suskin Ostriker, *Green Age*
Alicia Suskin Ostriker, *The Imaginary Lover*
Greg Pape, *Black Branches*
Greg Pape, *Storm Pattern*
Kathleen Peirce, *Mercy*
David Rivard, *Torque*
Liz Rosenberg, *Children of Paradise*
Liz Rosenberg, *The Fire Music*
Natasha Sajé, *Red Under the Skin*
Maxine Scates, *Toluca Street*
Ruth L. Schwartz, *Accordion Breathing and Dancing*
Robyn Selman, *Directions to My House*
Richard Shelton, *Selected Poems, 1969–1981*
Reginald Shepherd, *Some Are Drowning*
Betsy Sholl, *The Red Line*
Peggy Shumaker, *The Circle of Totems*
Peggy Shumaker, *Wings Moist from the Other World*
Jeffrey Skinner, *The Company of Heaven*
Cathy Song, *School Figures*
Leslie Ullman, *Dreams by No One's Daughter*
Constance Urdang, *Alternative Lives*
Constance Urdang, *Only the World*
Michael Van Walleghen, *Tall Birds Stalking*
Ronald Wallace, *People and Dog in the Sun*
Ronald Wallace, *Time's Fancy*
Belle Waring, *Refuge*
Michael S. Weaver, *My Father's Geography*
Michael S. Weaver, *Timber and Prayer: The Indian Pond Poems*
Robley Wilson, *Kingdoms of the Ordinary*
Robley Wilson, *A Pleasure Tree*
David Wojahn, *Glassworks*
David Wojahn, *Late Empire*
David Wojahn, *Mystery Train*
Paul Zimmer, *Family Reunion: Selected and New Poems*

The author and publisher wish to acknowledge the following publications in which some of these poems first appeared: *AGNI* ("Called Up: Tinker to Evers to Chance," "Mother Hunger and Her Seatbelt"); *Antioch Review* ("The Older Brothers of Girls I Grew Up With"); *Bakunin* ("The Nude Detective"); *Fine Madness* ("Shoestore Monkey"); *Graham House Review* ("Crow Sermon"); *Harvard Review* ("My Anger in 1934"); *Indiana Review* ("Some Questions We Might Ask"); *Michigan Quarterly Review* ("Surfing as Meditation"); *Parnassus: Poetry in Review* ("The Vinegarroon," "When I Think About America Sometimes (I think of Ralph Kramden)"); *Passages North* ("On the Poisoning of a Neighborhood Cat," "On First Looking into Wells Fargo and Seeing a Rock Star"); and *Sycamore Review* ("Shirts & Skins").

"The Jaws of Life" and "The Prodigal Daughter" first appeared in *The Gettysburg Review*, volume 8, number 1, and are reprinted here with permission of the editors.

"Some Questions We Might Ask" also appears in *Cape Discovery: The Fine Arts Work Center in Provincetown Anthology*.

Library of Congress Cataloging-in-Publication Data

Barresi, Dorothy 1957-
The post-rapture diner / Dorothy Barresi.
p. cm. —(Pitt Poetry Series)
ISBN 0-8229-3896-0 (cl.).—ISBN 0-8229-5581-4 (pbk.)
I. Title. II. Series.
PS3552.A7326P67 1995 95-21966
811'.54—dc20 CIP